SHEDS AND SHELTERS

by
Toni Webber

Illustrations by
Carole Vincer

THRESHOLD BOOKS

First published in Great Britain by
Threshold Books, The Kenilworth Press Limited,
661 Fulham Road, London SW6 5PZ

Typeset by Rapid Communications Ltd,
London WC1

Printed in England by Westway Offset

British Library Cataloguing in Publication Data
Webber, Toni
    Sheds and shelters.
    1. Livestock : Horses. Care
    I. Title II. Vincer, Carole
    636.1′083

    ISBN 0-901366-79-X

CONTENTS

Introduction

Few animals need quite as much storage space as ponies. Whether your horse is stabled for part of the time or lives out all the year round, you will soon find that you have acquired a vast quantity of general items that have to be put somewhere.

A horse or pony in a field needs some sort of protection from the worst of the weather, and this can range from a simple windbreak to a fully fledged shelter.

Hard food such as horse nuts, barley, chaff and bran must be stored in a dry, vermin-proof area. If your horse has supplements like cod liver oil or milk pellets, they must be kept close to the rest of the food. Hay, the most important part of his winter diet, must be kept under cover and readily accessible.

Saddles, bridles, rugs, bandages, travelling equipment and other valuable accessories must be given a storage area that is secure , while such things as the grooming kit, buckets, haynets and other items of everyday use have to be kept together, tidy and dry.

Fortunately for your pocket, you do not need a complete stable complex to satisfy all requirements. Garden sheds, garages, lean-tos, even household cupboards, can be pressed into service to keep your horse in the lap of luxury.

Do You Need a Field Shelter?

A field shelter is a three-sided shed erected in a field so that the ponies and horses occupying the field may go in and out of it as they please.

Unfortunately, the horses seem to spend most of their time outside, and their caring owners are often surprised when their beloved animals appear to ignore the shelter altogether. After going to so much trouble, the humans can be forgiven for wondering where they have gone wrong.

In fact, their only mistake is to ascribe human feelings to their horses. Cold does not worry them; they are indifferent to rain. The two elements which cause them the most distress and from which they will actively seek shelter are driving wind and a hot summer sun. At these times a field shelter undoubtedly has its uses.

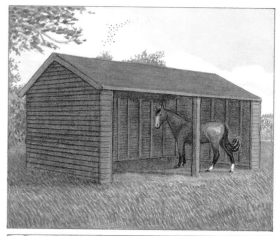

Even so, the interior of the shelter is likely to be occupied voluntarily only when the sun is at its height. As the top picture shows, a pony will then be grateful to the shed for the shade and freedom from flies that it offers. In strong winds and driving rain or snow, he is just as likely to shelter *behind* the shed as inside it (*centre*).

If removable bars are used to close off the opening, the shelter provides a useful pen in which to keep a pony for a short time. This can be particularly important in spring when a pony prone to laminitis must be isolated from the rich spring grass for a few hours each day. It is also useful in summer for a pony that suffers from sweet itch.

When planning where to site a field shelter, leave enough space for a horse to get behind it, and position it so that the opening is away from the prevailing wind and the full glare of the sun.

Types of Field Shelter

Field shelters are available from a number of manufacturers, who will supply them in sections and erect them on site. They are usually 12 feet (3.6 metres) deep and as wide as the customer requires.

Where there are a number of horses and ponies sharing a field, the shelter should be as large as possible. If one of the long sides is not to be kept completely open, it is most important to make the entrance wide, at least 8 feet (2.4m). A very large shelter could have two openings.

The roof can be single or double pitched. If a single pitch is chosen, it should slope from front to back.

Guttering is worth any extra expense; it can have a downpipe carrying the rainwater to a water trough. This should not be the only source of water available.

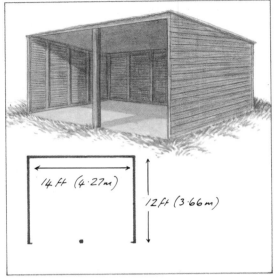

A small shelter may be left completely open or the roof may be supported by a single, centrally placed pole. A single pitched roof should slope from front to back.

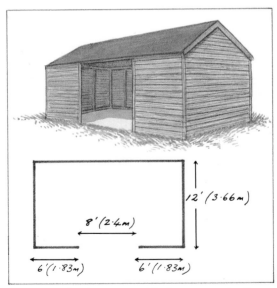

A wider shed can provide better protection for the horses if part of the opening is closed off. In this case, the doorway should be at least 8 feet (2.4m) wide.

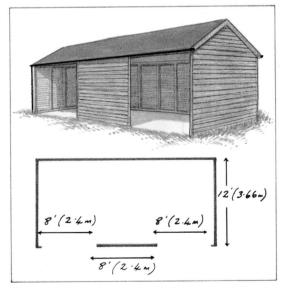

Very wide sheds can have two openings, with the boarded part placed centrally. For large sheds, pitched roofs are preferable; if necessary fitted with guttering.

Materials

A field shelter is not regarded as a permanent building and is usually built of timber, seasoned and treated.

Methods of anchoring it to the ground vary. The timber frame may be erected on a narrow plinth, built of concrete or of timber sleepers. Sleepers are secured by steel rods sunk deep into the ground. Sometimes the main posts themselves are driven into the soil. In most cases the framework is strengthened by cross members.

Walls are filled in with planking, either shiplap or tongue-and-groove, to give a sturdy, draught-free construction. A cheaper infill is half-round planking. The standard material for the roof is exterior-grade plywood, sealed with bitumen and covered with green mineral felt. An alternative is corrugated sheeting, securely fastened to the roof trusses.

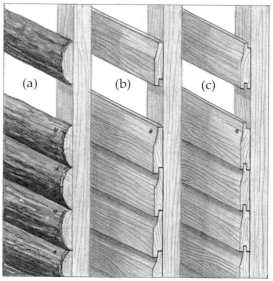

Wood is the most commonly used material for shelters. Three types of timber may be used for the walls: (a) rustic half-round; (b) shiplap; (c) tongue-and-groove.

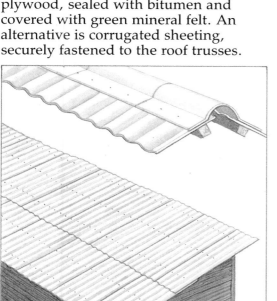

Roofs must be securely fastened down. The most inexpensive material is **corrugated metal** or **plastic sheeting** fixed under a ridge cover and overlapping as shown here.

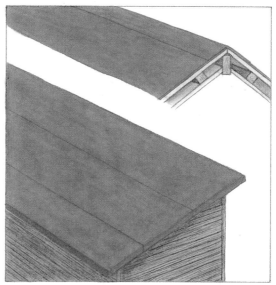

Though it is more expensive, green **mineral felt** gives a finer finish to the roof, looks better and is more durable. Most shed manufacturers recommend it for roofs.

Floors

It is not normally necessary to construct a floor for a field shelter, although some people prefer to lay down a concrete square the exact size of the shelter which stands on it. A concrete floor, if used, should be built with a slight slope towards the front, so that any water can drain away.

If the ground is left bare, however, the floor can get poached, particularly on a heavy clay soil, and it helps if you cover the ground with straw. The straw can be changed regularly or topped up to make a deep-litter bed.

Alternatively, a load of chalk, spread on the ground and rolled flat, improves the standing. Chalk drains well.

Timber sleepers, laid from front to back, make a very durable floor. If these are chosen, be sure to leave a ¼-inch (6mm) gap between the sleepers to provide drainage.

Floors inside field shelters tend to get very muddy if they are neglected. The simplest floor covering is **straw**, but it should be regularly cleaned out and replaced.

Chalk gives a quick-draining surface to a clay soil. Buy a load from a builder's merchant and spread it evenly over the ground, in and just outside the shed.

At greater expense, **railway sleepers** make a sound, durable flooring. They must be correctly laid, so that they do not rock, and have narrow gaps for drainage.

Fittings

Fittings in a field shelter should be kept to a minimum. Many horse owners, however, like to encourage their animals to use the shelter by feeding them inside it.

To prevent waste, it is best to place the hay in a rack or to provide haynets. The rack should be fixed to the back wall of the shelter at waist height.

Haynets need wall-mounted rings. Standard rings, made of galvanised iron, have two forms of attachment: a plate, which can be mounted on the wall with screws, and a bolt, which passes right through the wall and is secured by a nut and washer on the other side. Mount the rings at head-height so that the haynet can be tied well clear of the ground.

If you want to shut off the opening from time to time, the easiest method is to provide slip-rail holders.

As with loose boxes, fittings should be kept to a minimum. If hay is to be fed inside, a **hayrack** at waist height is a useful means of keeping it well clear of the ground.

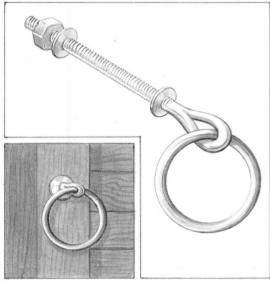

Rings to which haynets or the pony can be tied are extremely useful in a field shelter. If possible, use the type of fitting which can be bolted right through the wall.

Angle brackets enable the opening to be closed by slip rails. There must be a central supporting post. It is safest to use three rails.

Windbreaks – Natural and Man-made

Field shelters are convenient, but they are not vital. Wild horses do not have shelters nor do they make use of natural ones like caves. A roof over his head is not important to the average pony.

A horse will seek a windbreak. In a bleak field, a dip in the ground may be the best shelter he can find, and if even that small comfort is lacking he will turn his back to the wind, spread his tail and lower his head to protect his face from the harshness of the weather.

If you are judging the suitability of a field in which to keep horses, look for natural windbreaks. A hedge on the windward side is invaluable, especially if it is allowed to grow high and thick, and contains traditional hedging plants. If necessary, reinforce the base of the hedge with fencing but avoid the temptation to cut it back. Manicured hedges are fine for arable farming but

All ponies living out need some form of windbreak. Without one, a pony will turn his back to the prevailing wind and will keep warm by moving around.

Natural windbreaks include **hedges**. The best hedge contains blackthorn, hawthorn, beech, hazel and holly, which should be allowed to grow thick and tall.

A **dip in the ground** may be the only form of windbreak available. It looks bleak, but native ponies can derive considerable comfort from undulating ground.

not good for horses.

Without a suitable hedge, see if you can site the perimeter fence so that the side of an existing building forms part of the boundary. A horse will stand happily in the lee of a high wall.

As a last resort, erect an artificial windbreak. A close-boarded zigzag fence will provide shelter from whichever direction the wind blows.

Make sure that the supporting posts of the fence are sunk deep enough in the ground to prevent it from being blown over in a high wind. Use posts 8 feet (2.4m) long and dig post-holes 2 feet (60cm) deep. Give the posts a good soaking in wood preservative first; the best way is to stand each post upright in a tin of preservative for at least 48 hours, allowing the fluid to be absorbed by the wood. Nail the boarding to the arris rails so that the planks overlap.

The **side** of a **building** or barn which forms part of the boundary of the field provides excellent shelter from the prevailing wind if it is situated in the right place.

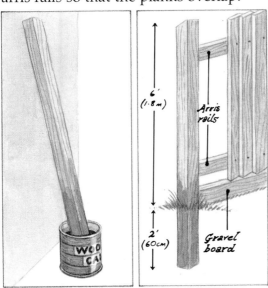

Before constructing the windbreak, **soak posts** in preservative, leaving them resting in the pot for up to a week. They need to be sunk 2 feet (60cm) into the ground.

If funds do not run to a full shelter, a **zigzag close-boarded fence**, 6 feet (1.8m) high, provides a suitable windbreak, which will be much used by the horses.

Alternative Shelters

If you cannot afford to buy a standard field shelter, a little ingenuity and do-it-yourself skill can produce a more than adequate alternative.

One fortunate horse owner had the opportunity of buying very cheaply an old railway wagon. He arranged for the wheels to be removed, and transported it to his horses' field, anchoring it to the ground with metal pegs. The door was taken off to provide an opening that was just the right size; and the interior was large enough to give his animals shelter from the sun.

Railway wagons, however, are not easy to come by, and you may well be tempted to seek something else.

If you have a suitable wall available, you could build a lean-to against it like the one shown opposite. For any do-it-yourselfer, reasonably competent at joinery and with the right tools, such a building is simple to erect.

The framework is made from sections of softwood, primed and painted to make it last, and the roof is covered with sheets of corrugated PVC.

A central post supports the roof at the front, and the two sides are filled in with overlapping planking.

The most difficult part of the construction is to get a satisfactory weatherproof seal between the back of the roof and the wall, but the problem can be overcome by using mineral felt as a flashing and a mastic seal for the join.

When looking around for suitable materials for a homemade shelter, do not use woven fencing panels, which are too flimsy, or corrugated iron, which has sharp edges. For reasons of safety, *never* use barbed wire or string to fix one section to another.

An effective field shelter is an old **railway wagon** without its wheels and laid flat on the ground. The opening is high and wide, but check the condition of the floor.

When building windbreaks *do not use* **fencing panels** or **corrugated iron** (which are too flimsy), **barbed wire** (too dangerous), or **string** (which breaks too easily).

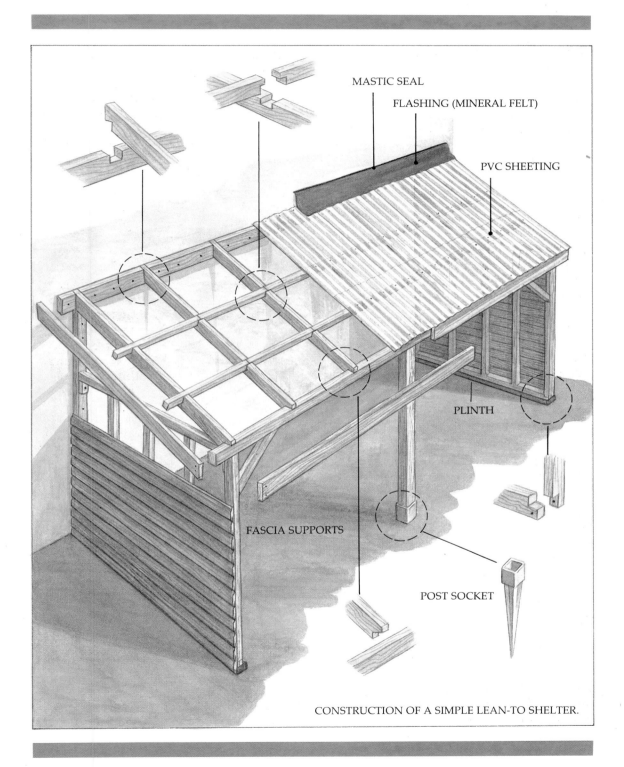

MASTIC SEAL

FLASHING (MINERAL FELT)

PVC SHEETING

PLINTH

FASCIA SUPPORTS

POST SOCKET

CONSTRUCTION OF A SIMPLE LEAN-TO SHELTER.

Feed Store

When planning storage for foodstuffs it is best to choose a place where they can all be kept together, with space for buckets and feed-bowls close to the food containers and a water tap near by.

A garden shed is ideal for a feed store as it has room for three or four cornbins and it is not too difficult to fit shelves for small items.

If you cannot spare a garden shed, try to make room in the garage. A line of bins along one wall, with shelving above, will still leave room for the car.

Alternatively, keep the bins under a small lean-to, where buckets can be stored as well. The lean-to protects the bins from the weather. If dustbins are used for the storage of hard food, it is best not to have them out in the open. On a blustery day, if a bin lid is blown off, the contents could be spoiled.

A **garden shed** makes a good store for hard feed, giving plenty of room for cornbins and buckets to be stowed away safely. Shelves for smaller items are easily fixed.

As an alternative, 'borrow' a corner of the **garage**. There is usually space inside for the bins and small pieces of equipment, but it must be kept as tidy as possible.

The simplest storage for bins and buckets is a simple **lean-to**. Try to avoid spillage of feedstuffs which will attract vermin. Rats can quickly contaminate exposed feed.

Almost all hard feed needs to be dampened down, so an outside **tap** is essential. Keep buckets close at hand, and store a hosepipe coiled up on the wall near-by.

Hard feeds must have vermin-proof containers. The cheapest are **dustbins**. Label clearly: sugar-beet pellets are easy to confuse with pony nuts.

Simple industrial **shelving** provides storage space for feed supplements, scales, etc. The shelving can be placed anywhere, but preferably as close to feedbins as possible.

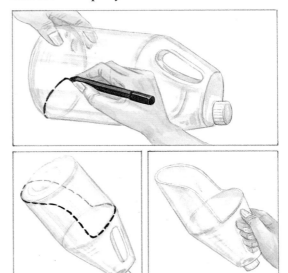

Make your own **scoop**, using a 2-litre plastic squash bottle. First, mark off the shape with a felt pen, then cut carefully round the dotted line as shown.

Hay Store

The cheapest way of buying hay is straight off the field. A full winter's supply can be obtained this way at half the price of buying it at intervals. It is, however, both bulky and difficult to store, and you would need a very large shelter to keep sufficient hay in stock for, say, two horses from late September to early May.

The best store is a barn with big double doors through which the bales can be easily unloaded. The bottom layer of bales should be supported on wooden pallets, which allow air to circulate underneath and prevent the bales from going mouldy.

An empty garage is an effective alternative and this would have room to keep enough hay for two ponies throughout the winter. A Dutch barn has room for several tons of hay, but its main disadvantage is that it has open sides and the outer layer of bales will soon become unusable unless you buy cheap straw bales and make protective walls from them.

For anyone without access to a large empty building, the only alternative is to have a regular order throughout the winter for small amounts of hay. An old skip turned on its side is extremely useful for this purpose as it can hold about eight bales.

If you build a small lean-to for the hay, do make certain that it is completely rainproof. Even a slight drip will quickly damage the hay unless it is being used very quickly.

If you have to store hay outside it must be raised on pallets and covered with waterproof sheeting. With a concrete base, one row of pallets would be sufficient, but two rows would be needed if the area is grassed.

Small quantities of hay can be kept outside in simple shelters, but ensure that the bales are raised on **pallets**, protected by a tarpaulin. An old **skip** would be suitable.

A **Dutch barn** will store a large amount of hay but the outside bales will deteriorate unless they are guarded from the weather. **Straw bales** make cheap protective walls.

A fully enclosed **barn** is the best hay store. As long as it has double doors, delivery of large loads is simple. Keep doors in good condition so that they shut easily.

A **garage** provides ample room for a winter's supply of hay for two ponies. Stack the bales criss-cross fashion, like laying bricks, for stability.

Even in an enclosed building, the hay should be raised off the ground by using wooden **pallets**. The pallets allow air to circulate underneath and prevent mould.

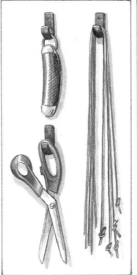

Hang accessories on **wall-mounted hooks** – penknife and scissors for cutting baler twine, discarded twine for use as string and, of course, spare haynets.

Tack Room

When you first acquire a horse or pony, the amount of tack is fairly small and easy to store: a saddle, bridle and headcollar can be kept in your bedroom, for example. After a while, however, the various items of tack tend to build up until even the most long-suffering mother will draw the line at using the bedroom as a store.

If you have stables, the tack room usually forms part of them. This is an excellent arrangement, as the tack and its wearer are then all in one place. A good alternative for home storage is a small garden shed, which can be equipped with all the fixtures necessary.

Without an individual tack room and where storage has to be at home, a spare cupboard may be the answer. The space under the stairs, awkwardly shaped though it may be, usually has room for most equipment.

Tack can find storage room in a variety of places. A simple, lockable **garden shed** is very suitable as it has room for brackets, hooks and storage trunks and boxes.

It is most convenient to have a room as part of the **stable complex**, and many manufacturers combine a tack room and a loose box as a package deal.

If space is tight, somewhere inside the house will have to be found. With careful planning an **understairs cupboard** will accommodate most items of equipment.

Fixtures . . .

If you have a tack room big enough for more than simple storage, it makes sense to think about the fixtures which are worth installing.

A sink or wash-basin is well worthwhile. Most metalwork needs scrubbing at some stage, and a line of hooks above the basin provides hanging space for the clean bits and irons.

Safe heating is another asset, so one or two power outlets should be installed. The heating system could consist of a simple blow-heater, an electrically operated oil-filled radiator, or a wall-mounted thermo-tube.

Heating helps to banish dampness and makes the room a pleasant place in which to clean tack; and it is also useful for drying out rugs. For this purpose, you could use a freestanding clothes horse or a ceiling airer operated by a rope and pulley.

The ideal tack room contains a number of items not usually found in small sheds. Ceiling and free-standing **airers** prevent rugs from getting musty and mildewed.

Safe forms of **heating** include a wall-mounted thermo-tube, a fan-heater and an oil-filled radiator. The tube and the radiator are cheap to run and can be left unattended.

A **sink** is useful for washing tack. It need not have a hot water supply, although hot water is best for cleaning bits and irons. Fix some drainage hooks above the sink.

. . . and Fittings

Every tack room needs fittings for storing equipment tidily and safely. Racks are needed for saddles, hooks for bridles, shelves and boxes for small items and rugs.

Saddles should always be kept on racks, either wall-mounted or floor-standing for individual saddles, or on a pole suspended between two supports where more than one saddle can be placed.

Bridles need wide brackets – *never* nails or narrow hooks – to prevent the leatherwork from bending too sharply and cracking. Rugs not in regular use should be kept in a trunk or suitcase, never piled on the floor.

The tack room is a good place for the first-aid cabinet. It is best to have a wall-mounted one.

Finally – and most important – an outside tack room needs a strong lock.

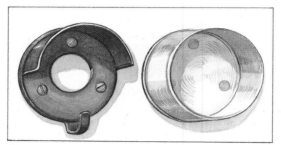

Bridle hooks: ready made and home-made. An empty baked-bean tin, painted, or a piece of circular log are excellent alternatives to custom-built fittings.

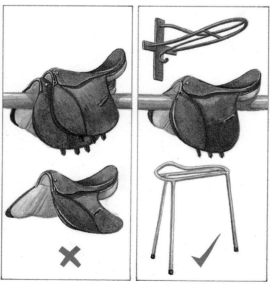

Store saddles on **racks**, either wall-mounted or free-standing, or on a pole suspended between chairs. Never place one saddle on top of another or flat on the floor.

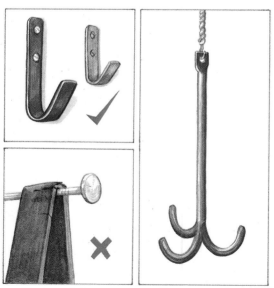

Leatherwork hung on a nail may crack. Use **wide hooks** rather than single nails. A **swivel hook** is useful for tack cleaning but should not be used for storage.

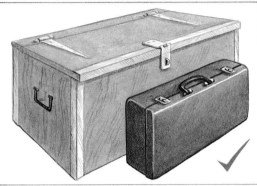

Never store rugs on the floor: they might get damp. It is better to keep them in an old **chest** or **suitcase** with mothballs. Never put them away damp.

Whips are easily lost. A home-made **whip-rack** will keep them safe. Cup-hooks attached to strips of wood provide better storage than hanging whips from loops.

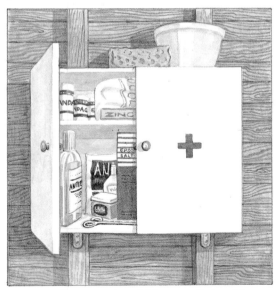

Every tack room should have a **first-aid cabinet**, accessible and containing items which store well and might be needed. Label scissors 'For first-aid only'.

Guard against theft with a heavy **padlock** or **rim-lock** on the tack-room door. The latter is safest as padlocks can be more easily forced. Keep the keys in a safe place.

Maintenance

Whether your shelters and sheds are expensive, custom-built affairs or home-made adaptations, careful maintenance is needed to keep them in a safe and weatherproof condition.

Get into the habit of looking around your shed or building from time to time, making a note of minor repairs to be done. Then ensure that you find the time to carry out those repairs before they become major ones. At least once a year give exterior woodwork a coat of preservative, paint or varnish.

The signs of wear and tear may be quite small. Planking nails can rise and screws can become loose. It takes only a few minutes to replace them or drive them home, but if you leave them unattended you could end up having to replace a whole section of woodwork.

Do not wait until the frosts of winter come before you lag outside piping and renew tap washers, or the drip will become a flood. Check all electrical fittings. Frayed cable, worn flex and damaged insulation are dangerous and can cause a fire. Fit rubber plugs to all electrical equipment which is to be used out of doors.

Keep an eye on all woodwork which is exposed to the weather. If there is any sign of rot – flaking or spongy wood – the offending section should be cut out and replaced.

Wooden doors need special attention. Hinges can become loose, particularly if the door is a close fit and the wood swells in wet weather. If necessary, remove the door and shave a sliver off the base. Always support the door on wedges when re-hanging it.

Look for small tears in roofing felt. Bitumen painted over the tear will prevent the damage from spreading.

Points to look out for: **nails** and **screws**. Check that nails securing boarding have not risen. Bang them home or replace. Tighten screws with a screwdriver.

Dripping **taps** (*left*) need new washers. Lag the pipes against frost. Check that **electric cable** and **light bulb fittings** are still serviceable. *Wire plugs correctly.*

Test with a screwdriver for signs of **wet rot** in timber. If wood is spongy, it should be replaced with fresh pieces liberally treated with wood preservative.

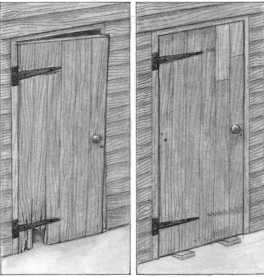

Doors may sag or rot in places. If necessary, replace with new wood and re-hang. Vulnerable areas are around the hinges and at the edges of doors.

Creosote or other preservative should be applied to woodwork regularly. Before treating exterior woodwork, wash down with anti-fungal solution and leave to dry.

If **roofing felt** becomes torn, first tack down the torn bits, then treat with bitumen. Larger tears must be patched with pieces of felt, using wide-headed roofing nails.

Emergency Shelter for a Sick Pony ■ ■ ■

For many pony-owners a stable is not a necessity. Throughout their period of owning a pony, they may never need to keep him in for any length of time.

Nevertheless, emergencies can happen. If a pony picks up a virus, undergoes a bout of colic, or suffers an accident for which a period of stable-rest is prescribed, a stable may be called for at very short notice.

On this sort of occasion, the first action to take is to telephone horsey friends to see if anyone has a spare stable to offer. Nine times out of ten, accommodation can be found.

It is when all else has failed that you have to consider the best temporary way of keeping your pony bedded down in warmth and comfort until he has recovered.

The first – indeed, probably the only – possibility is to make use of a garage, which, without its usual occupant, has all the space a sick pony could possibly need. Prepare the garage with care.

First of all, remove all sharp and angular objects such as mowers, garden tools, tins of paint, etc. Take down any shelves below head-height, and cover windows with chicken wire. Then, most important of all, sweep the floor thoroughly to remove any bits of débris, old nails, pieces of wire, splinters of wood, etc., until the floor is absolutely clean.

Ask your local farmer for straw, and make a thick, soft bed, piling the straw up around the sides. If possible, reduce the length of the garage by making a barrier of straw bales. As the pony gets better, this barrier can be reinforced with a 'swinging bale', a length of wood suspended from the roof beams by ropes.

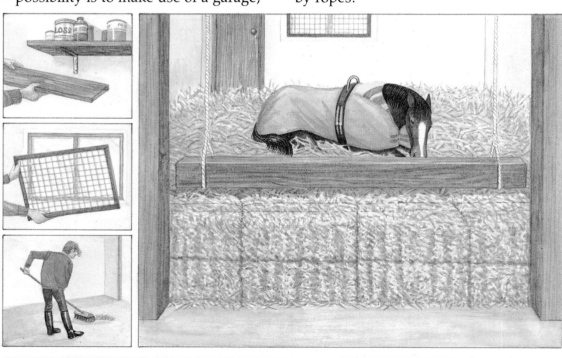